Female Superiority

by S.A.I. Steve Lando

Monogamy bores me terrible. I prefer polygamy and polyandry.
I am a tamer of men, a cat, an Italian
Carla Bruni

The gender difference

a guy is always easy to satisfy
a goddess, however, needs to get it all, and then more

Homo sapiens biblica femina

You are the apex of the evolution

first was the earth created
then the nature
the animals
the man
and then finally you women

the best always come last

Homo sapiens biblica femina

as I now and then have proclaimed
a woman's right to pleasure always comes first
an inborn entitlement to more partners exists

if necessary, she could also lie about it
this is plain and clearly supported
of God and church

tho, Mary's sexual escapades by him was protected
surely no sensible person believes,
that God actually was Jesus' father,
although Joseph the wimp so imagined

tho, we now live in a modern world
we should surely be more mature than that,
so why not just admit your divine right

Maria
you go before all else

Homo sapiens biblica femina

when Adam took his bite
went it not down
but hooked on

when Eve took her bite
it slipped down in a bit

the whole piece was obtained
in full vigor

ready to take another bite

for she is not satisfied
on just a little bit

the divine nature has made its choice
let the woman get what to her belong

as much as she wants
forbidden fruit or not

Sex education: Control of Procreation of Children

one of the most common theoretical explanation models in sociobiology and anthropology for a large part of the communities of the world, has been that women are socially and culturally forced into monogamic relationships because that the male should be able to control that it really are his children, she gives birth to

now in modern times it is so that the woman herself with potency could control whose child she give birth to, using birth control pills and day after pills, or through other means, thus there is absolutely no biological reason why women on the basis of the above common explanation should live in a monogamic relationship

on the contrary, the man cannot control who he has a child with if he lives in a non-monogamic manner, condoms can break and otherwise he is dependent on the trust and guarantees of the sexual partner, which of course, for obvious reasons, not always are relying

so based on these aspects, and many many more, it is self-evident that the woman, in a relationship, may require a monopoly of the man's seed and lust, while she is free to lust herself with others

Female pleasure

is the essence of creation

Power of Desire

You women, thou
own us in total

for our manhood
our phallus
pulsates with desire and longing

thus giving you all the power in the world
to master us in total
just as it should be

if one devotes oneself to goddess worship
which I think one should

Your Pleasure

You girls,

you are sacred creations
wandering this earth so beauteous

your happiness and pleasure
our desire towards Ye

is written in the stars
the contract is made

we are here for You

you should sit on a pedestal
receive all you so want
enjoy to the full

our desire is Yours alone
you could be desired by all you want

do you want more
get to enjoy who you want
so is it, so it should be
our desire is total

your pleasure, is sacral

the choice, is yours

Your pleasure

Your innermost self

Your inner wild
Your divine self

Your inner lusts
should be affirmed

in the name of sacrality

both You and I
Your inner fulfillment
desire to affirm

I so
for the lust
I to You so
feel

You so
for that You
Your inner self
wish to fulfill

Your inner divinity
Yourself primarily see

Your divine I
I primarily see

We both realize
that Your pleasure
must primarily come

through your pleasure
we both pleasure feel

Hence I thee
no pleasure could deny
I would then your I strongly smear

your wildly I
as we both so worship

Goddess

I worship your excellent creation
recognizing its complexity

I love and crave your inner
as well as your outer

I love and totally burn up
in my desire when I get to taste your taste
both from thy fjord of amour
as sipping gently along thy skin

Your pleasure and satisfaction
both spiritual, mental as physical
means everything for me
I hope it does so
for you as like

without any shackles
or veil over your soul

You own

you own my sexuality
my phallus

my orgasm

Free satisfactions

seeing a pleased woman's eyes
is true satisfaction for one's entity
when she has it all

seeing a lustful women's glance
is ecstatic in it's true shape
when she wants more

seeing a pleasured woman's visage
is to see the fructification of paradise
when she gets more

Angel girl

as a princess, angel
queen and goddess

you should live

Spoiled

spoiled by birth
you should always be

the whcle life

All women

I believe in making a woman like you, feel like the goddess you deserve, all the time.

Your Excellency

I can't help it, but I find you excellent, divine excellent
it's nothing odd about it, women are the best, You deserve it all

The most beautiful

You are the most beautiful mind, the most beautiful person, captured in the most beautiful body, that's the most beautiful incarceration you can imagine, but You are correct, You should let be totally free, free in your mind, free in your body, free to do whatever you like, and wish

to be your slave, is the most beautiful position one could have, as a man

Slavery

to be your slave, is the most beautiful position one could have, as a man

Paradise taste

inside paradise
tasting

Your divine soul

Pleasures

your pleasure
multiples in me

every drop of it

Drops of the Goddess

white cloud mountains
tops that seeps
land that licks

in freedom it bears

Fjord of amour

when one tastes your firth

where salt meets sweet
where tongue meets lips
where creation is

the taste of the sky

Kneeling

from toe to top
bending down

before You

Kissing feet

you worshiped goddess
I kiss the feet of you
these lovely goodies

in veneration of you, my goddess
you graceful woman

Desire

a goddess emittings
of aphoristic fluids

rose water of the soul

my mental elixir of life
my soul's desire

you watering my mouth

Heavenly addictions

so let the saltiness of you
drip into the mouth of me

tasting goddessly you do

The taste of You

I can not help it

but with you in my thought, with the movement of my fingers along your skin, with the tongue there closely, slowly going ahead, tasting your entity

giving me a heavenly euphoric feeling, intimately as such, with both my mind and heart in ecstasy, pulsing ahead

Bacchic amour

tenderness in the heart
libation of love
one's heart is caressed

licking one's mind
til ecstasy is enshrined

with taste of divinity
euphoria can be felt
drink of love tasted

libation of love
heart's delight

plowed sensuousness
in furrow of eternity

Amphitrite, god who has you

with the salt in your womb's port
I swim into your arm's court

taste the entity of your soul
within Poseidon's glorious hole

Ensouling love

rolling the pearl
with the help of my mouth
by my tongue

gives you the pleasure of a blissful event
so that you reach the height of ecstasy
the body of yours get satisfied

giving you amour of the deepest descent
from the soul's precipitous depth
so that your mind becomes satisfied
and happiness reaches the maximum height

your soul's happiness
is my soul's prime delight

Dreams delight

you bring dream life to paradise height
with your words that become my joy

in your paradise, one gets to taste your nectar
for all time to come
where I of course, therefore, would like to come
inbreathe your lovely flower

Nectar

every inch of You
is totally sacral

every drop of You
is totally sacral

Yoni Goddess

the enigma of Your soul
Your body, Your nectar

every inch of You
is totally sacral

every drop of You
is totally sacral

the sacrality of your body
a body of the universe

a pussy like a star

Life

the enigma of Your soul
Your body, Your nectar

Tasting

let me lick taste your nectar
making me your slave

Pussylover

wanting to taste your orgasm
your fluids of pleasure

your euphoria
your ecstasy

your soul

Nectar

~I~

your inner fluids
sow the taste of divinity
when I so them taste

Nectar

I fulfill my inner
with the nectar thou me giveth
the one I so seek

I want to taste thee
in everlasting time

Nectar

nectar from your pleasure
the soul's bodily fluids of the Divine

I will taste, anytime

Your

nectar of pleasure
upfilling my mouth

divine juice

Holiest of the holy

your opening to your
sacral soul

where, the nectars flow

Les femmes de fleur

power to the flower
the divine nectar is in You

Nectar

the drops of You
shaped cf Your soul

ecstasic, when Ycu feel so

Garden of Eden

the gate of life
the tongues of mouth

the meadow of Heaven

Nectar

your inner fluids
sow the taste of divinity
when I them taste

those from the eyes outflowing at joy
those from the mouth outtrickling when tongues swirl
those from the the fjord of amour secreted whence tasted

I fulfill my inner
with the nectar thou me giveth
the one I so seek

I want to taste thee
in everlasting time

thy soul

Wine

sipping your wine
thine nectar

me tasting divine

Goddess

You are the Goddess
You are the Sun

You are the Light

Worship

You are the Goddess
You are the Sun

You are the Light

in spirit, in mind
in body, in essence

You should be worshiped
by yourself, by us, by everyone

Worshiped

in spirit, in mind
in body, in essence

You should be worshiped
by yourself, by us. by everyone

Girl

you are a girl
a Goddess

i am a boy
a nobody

You are worth it All

Slave

I'll be the slave of the goddess
I obey

what ever you say

The moon and stars

if he is willing to give you
the moon and stars

you should demand
the whole universe

you are worth it all
not just some bits of it

Women rulers

women rulers
women warriors

women goddesses

Woman's look

to look into Heaven
you see the Goddess

and cannot never return

I like it

when You are a tigress
taking what You want

however you want

Behave

she doesn't need to behave
she just needs to do

what the hell she wants

Men's opinion

men's opinion
mens feelings

are totally irrelevant

Power over Man

I obey truthfully
licking Your feet

loyal and obedient
faithfully

while You
enjoy Men

Small dick humiliatoin

is the funniest thing

Reginal power

All Woman are Goddesses
and all Men should worship Her

in full, and totally, loyal and faithful

Women should be free to reign
in full power, in full freedom

The first Gender, the first Person, the first Life

the fetal brain begins in a *female* typical state

the presence of the Y-chromosome in males
prompts the development of testes, which release testosterone

to masculinize the fetus and fetal brain

Lesbian couple

just put a cock cage on him
use him as a slave

domestical and economical

Why Women should have Several Men

it is so
that the trail of evolution
made so that women several men
should let in, in her self
this I have always known, in myself

when the man the competition feels
when the woman several men fucks
wrathful jealousy should not his mind fuel
without the side effects, he should fess up

with the desire of the woman
as the goddess she really is

the wish that with her
have children, from this fertility goddess
using his own pole

with swimming spermies
of top quality
creating children for academies
no bloody wannabies

the woman should get
to have sex with other yet

for the children's sake if nothing else than so[1]

---

[1] Writing based on an experiment featured in the British scientific journal *Biology Letters*, 050608, which shows that the quality of sperm significantly increases when their proprietors actively sees a naked woman with two other men, compared to 'just' see a naked woman.

Sensuality

a sensual woman can not be cheating
she is only true to her sensuality

The Free Nature

to adore nature
and let other people know about it

to adore wildering woman
and let other people know about it

to adore the goddess
the divinity of nature

Wildness

the wildness in your body
should let grow free, breathe freely

wild free

Wildly

you are a wild animal
a tigress. You should be let free

roaming wild

Ride freely

ride freely, ride lovely
liberate body and soul

let the goddess within you
take what she wants

My religion

to taste You

to taste your
tears of joy

your skin
your lips
your liquids of pleasure

your soul's nectar
your happiness, your enjoyment

is time of blessedness

Divine

In all your life, this is You, the Divine

Women

the primal force
the heart of life

the energy
of the universe

Worship

everyday

I would like to tell you
that You are my goddess

Girls

magic as such
magnificent even more

worshiped they must

Women

the primal force
the heart of life

the energy
of the universe

magic as such
magnificent even more

worshiped she must

So fine

You're just so fine
You don't need to be kind

You are a Goddess

Obedience

everyday

I would like to tell you
that I am your slave

Wild horse

divine you
goddess you

natural wild
in gallop

should let ride free
how and when you want

your inner strength
your inner wildness

must not be bridled
or forgoing

but, ridden

Sacrality

the sacrality of your body
a body of the universe

Yoni

the sacrality of your body
a body of the universe

a pussy like a star

Sacredness

the sacrality of your body
a body of the universe

every inch of You
is totally sacral

every drop of You
is totally sacral

the enigma of Your soul
Your body, Your nectar

Pussy Power

Power to the Flower
life's ænigma is in You

Power to the Girls
life's ænigma is in You

Power to the Pussy
life's ænigma is in You

Pussy Riot

Power to the Flower
the divine nectar is in You

Power to the Girls
life's ænigma is in You

Power to the Pussy
life's universe takes root in You

Women

born to rule the World

Woman

born to rule the World

every day, every night
every moment in our existence

is about serving the Higher Good
the Goddess of the Almighty Being

in every woman's soul

Men

born to Serve

Female supremacy

male are built
to obey, and serve

bring joy
and adore

Female supremacy

we men exists
for being used by you

for You

Being your dog

I follow you around loyally

loving you truthfully
licking your feets

worshiping you

but I will cuddle like a cat

Pussy power

dogs have masters
cats have servants

pussies we obey

Feminine power

Women are the primal force, Women are the heart of the whole life cycle, Women are the maintainers of the life force, and should be protected and honoured for that fact, her power is magic and magnificent, who aught to be worshiped as the natural force she is, as the Goddess, of the Moon, tripartite face thereof, the Divine, the Diane

Femdom paradise

good girls may go to heaven
but the bad girls own the place

heaven and earth
it's all Yours

in the paradise
of freedom

Unicorn

the only correct religion that exists
is that of You, as a Goddess

Dancing Moon

be like a Goddess
because that is what You are

dance wild and be free

Be Yourself

be proud of who you are
just be yourself

the Goddess You are

Night shining moon

as the Goddess of clear spring day
as the Goddess when the moon shines night

I like You to have, pleasure of the sky

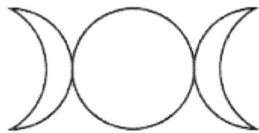

Ashteroth

Queen of Heaven
Lady of the Sea

Tree of Life

Sacred Pole
in a Grove

Goddess of Motherhood
and Sexuality

Your fluids

taste like
heaven and clouds

taste like
a Goddess

which You are

Yonilover

wanting to

taste your orgasm
your fluids of pleasure

your euphoria
your ecstasy

your soul

Your devotée

Your devotée
at Your service

all the time
always

You Goddess

You are every man's dream

anyone whom You catches
will stay with You, forever

loving You
adoring You
worshiping You

tasting You

Devotion

Your devotée
at Your service

all the time
always

You Goddess

Pussie's power

you got the pussy
you are divine

you should be on top

he below

Unbridled

curb nothing
you should not be restrained at all

bite freely, lust yowling

Femme-in-ism

free-dom
fem-dom

dôm-in-femme

forbidden fruit
the essence of flowers

woman of pleasure

Drops of the Goddess

white clad mountains
tops that seeps
land that licks

in freedom it bears

God(dess mine)

as nuns & monks
I give

my sexuality
my emotions
my senses
my thoughts
my worship
my love
my desire
my self

to You

as nuns & monks
I request not
that thou only should belongst to me

thou canst not so do
thou art of divine nature
thou art a goddess

there exist no God
besides You

to forsake everyone's love
everyone's desire
to you

is to deny humanity
the best there is

to forsake your right

to satisfaction
to reverence
to love
to desire

is to deny you
the best there is

as nuns & monks
I am happily included
in your harem
in your stable

tho we all aren
thanks to a goddess like thou

as nuns & monks
I become fulfilled by your existence
of your essence
to be a part, of your all

the totality that thou art worth
consisting of
You, goddess, in its core

the Queen

a she-cats pleasure always comes first
and should so do both for her as the other
this should all think

a she-cat willingly receives caresses and cuddling
not only from one, I mean why?

a she-cat is manipulative, or may be
she often goes to the neighbour for cuddling
without saying anything

a she-cat should be desired, worshiped, loved, caressed
without deviation, other than that is not tolerable

she is a true predator,
and the best creature on this earth

yes I am only a guy
genetically engineered, to desire the she-cat
what else can I do
what else want I do

there is nothing more desirable than the she-cat
one melts of her merely entity

precisely all for your delight
free for you to enjoy
which you also so should

Sound of a harp

one feels the vibes from you
shining as a whole goddess
one of the few, with the extra pedigree

one melts so before you
there is nothing, nothing at all

that would get me to say no
to anything at all, you wanted or desired

your whole formation, essence
must always be let to beget

every cell in your creation
· must act for achieving satisfaction
and more thereto

to belittle, forsake, forbid this
had been do darken your inner light

and not am I, to wish its quenching

Goddess eyes

your beautiful dark
fulfilling eyes

one finds oneself
staring into
the bosom of eternity

weak-kneed one melts
in front of your admirable entity

bowing until one reaches
the harbour of thy fjord of amour

tasting the saltiness
that your soul consists of
essence of the universe

Your breasts

your beautiful flowers
to breast

spreading nectar to
your child

this perfect creation
on your divine creature

we cannot otherwise do
than to love in full

Hot source of Life

soul essential lovemaking
whirling fjords of amour

swimming in paradise

woman
young lady • veneration
fineness • godlike • dedication
doubtless • fondness • diamond • decoration
greater • deification • dignity
fallow • morning star
goddess

That is how it is

a total erotic experience
spiritually satisfactory
with the senses rushing
to seventh heaven

viewing the goddess in her eyes

Prayer

you free goddess
your pleasure is sacral
lust is your ethos

I pray on my knees
that you get everything you want
and I at least become a part

Impossibilities

there is no possibility
to do anything else

than adore, love, and desire

You

Divinity

You should feel yourself
You are the best there is

You are Divine

Divine

in freedom
in totality
in waves

of emotions

your feelings lusts
your hands freedom
your hearts beats
your lusts sea

your ecstasies
your euphoria

is totally sacred

thou est Divinal

Rule of Queen

You rule our world
as it should be

facesitted by a Queen

Power over Men

we all know that women really have all the power over men
and that is precisely as it should be

Demanding

you should always demand to receive more
even if you are together with one guy

Your value

you are worth nothing less than all
and You should have it

You

may be totally free
free to love and have sex

feel pleasure and enjoyment

freely from wherever

Variation

You must absolutely have variation, every woman's physique, mind, body, heart and soul, needs to get variation - enjoy, enjoy, enjoy, enjoy!

Your demands and wishes

should be respected and adored
worshiped and innerly accepted

Your wish

is my wish

A Woman's Wishes

a woman should always be free to do anything she wants
a man should always do anything she wants

Goddess Girl's relationships

A true man does never think that You are boring when You are yourself, a woman like You are the goddess of all man's imagination, he will look upon You with his eyes and mind totally beloved and inloved in Your very essence.

A woman like You could also try to show a strong appearance, that You are loved by many, that You are appreciated by many, that many men adore You and feel Your sensuelle look - that You are a femme fatale, a catwoman. He does not own you, You own him.

A true man will get down on his knees to kiss Your feet, anytime, he will let You rule his mind, and let You freely lust around, although he himself will be totally faithful before You - You should have the freedom to enjoy other, and he will worship You like the gooddess You are.

You cannot be boring, in any man's mind, because You are not boring.
You have to believe in Your self, and he will do the same.

You are a Goddess, nothing less.

You should not be all to nice, let him fight for You, not the other way around. You got the power, you got the pussy, *it's pussy power*, You are divine, You should be on top, of him, that will make him want You, for ever.

A true man loves you, without that You do anything else, then being Yourself, a Goddess.

He should show You his love for You all the time, he should always do everything for You, Your pleasure and enjoyment should always be the highest priority of his mind - in Your

132

relationship You should always be free to do anything you want, with anybody, or when ever, you want, and You should always be free to not need to do anything that You do not want to do - he should always do anything You want him to do, all Your demands and wishes should be respected and adored, worshiped and innerly accepted, Your wish, is his wish.

As Aphrodite, You must be totally free for free love and sex, pleasure and enjoyment, he should never be free, he should be totally truthful and loyal to You, only worshiping, loving and adoring, You.

Any longstanding relationship with a Goddess like You must be like this, You must enjoy it totally, and get the maximum of everything.

The Truth of You

You should stay as You are, real to Yourself and Your inner soul therein is the real truth for everything, and every question You might have

You have the truth, You are the truth

The Truth

Thou hast the truth, Thou art the truth
In all Thy life, Thou best Divine

The Truth

Thou hast the truth, Thou art the truth

Priorities

the pleasure of You
is always on the highest priority

of our minds

Togetherness

a girl could always get more
so she should get more

a guy could always give more
so he should give more

Woman

should receive
it all

not the least in the bed, where you have the right to enjoy everybody you want, but also receive it all from your lovers, truthfully and loyal

Keyholder

women in charge
men in cages

When women take control

men obey

Joie de vivre

your thirst of pleasure
your pursuit of pleasure

reigns supreme

Joie de vivre

your thirst of pleasure
your pursuit of pleasure

reigns supreme

euphoria,
should be your mode of mind

Girl Power

Power to the Girls
life's ænigma is in You

Flower Power

Power to the Flower
the divine nectar is in You

Power to the Girls
life's ænigma is in You

Power to the Pussy
our tongues are in You

Worshiping

on our knees we stand
worshiping You

As Goddesses

every girl should be treated as such
as the Goddesses You really are

on our knees we stand
worshiping You

Your essence

every little bit of your essence
is sacral

every little bit of your essence
is divine

Essences

every little bit of your essence
is sacral

every little bit of your essence
is divine

every little bit of my essence
is your slave

A Goddess like You

should always receive pleasure
should always receive Amour

without boundaries
your soul must be free

we could not do
anything, than ye adore

A Goddess like You

should always receive pleasure

receive everything that You want
everything that You like

receive everything You adore
everything that makes You happy

should always receive Amour

without boundaries
Your soul must be free

we could not do
anything, than adore Ye

Ye

free in Your mind
free in Your body

free to do

Goddess

free to do

whatever You wish
whatever You like

You are

free to do
what you want

all the time

Free

in love and sex
and everything else

all the time

A woman's wish

a woman should always be free to do anything she wants
and be free to not do those things, she does not want

Woman

should receive
it all

My Goddess

I am your worshiper
my goddess

I am Your slave

Adored

You, and all women, should be
respected, adored, and totally worshiped
as the Goddesses You truly are

Worshiping truth

we are made to serve, adore
love and worship

women

You own

my mind
my soul
my body

Flying Free

flying free

in every aspect of your life
in every essence of your soul

flying free

in your heart
in your body

in your pleasures

Freedom

totally free, You

free in Your mind
free in Your body

free to do

whatever You wish
whatever You like

Self-esteem

Your self-esteem should be as high as possible
You have the right to feel like a goddess

in every way, on every day

Working for You

women should actually have the total power over men, that you really receive nothing less than all, and that we do everything for you, in our worshiping souls and bodies, working for You

You must

receive everything that You want, everything that You like
receive everything You adore, everything that makes You happy

Nice girl

You should not be all to nice, let him fight for You, not the other way around. You got the power, you got the pussy, *it's pussy power*, You are divine, You should be on top, of him, that will make him want You, for ever.

Worshiping man

A true man will get down on his knees to kiss Your feet, anytime, he will let You rule his mind, and let You freely lust around, although he himself will be totally faithful before You - You should have the freedom to enjoy other, and he will worship You like the goddess You are.

Freedom and Love

You should have the freedom to enjoy other
I will worship You like the goddess thou art

Believe

You have to believe in Your self, and he will do the same
You are a Goddess, nothing less

You

you have the right
to feel like a goddess

in every way, on every day

As You Wish

Everything this, and everything at all, is about your self-esteem and self-confidence, if you feel like a goddess, and men, and women, appreciate you as a goddess, see you as a person with strong aura, all persons will melt down before you, worship and adore you.

Not any heterosexually man will ever tell you the words 'no' to you, what ever you want, what ever you desire, what ever you demand.

Being yourself

A good man loves you, without that You do anything else, then being Yourself, a Goddess.

Showing Love

He should show You his love for You all the time, he should always do everything for You, Your pleasure and enjoyment should always be the highest priority of his mind - in Your relationship You should always be free to do anything you want, with anybody, or when ever, you want, and You should always be free to not need to do anything that You do not want to do - he should always do anything You want him to do, all Your demands and wishes should be respected and adored, worshiped and innerly accepted, Your wish, is his wish.

Doing things

no need for You
to do anything

that a man can do
for You

Liberties

I am very glad that you agree that women should bee free, having full liberties, especially concerning love and sex, which is very important for your enjoyment and self-esteem, but I would say you also would need liberties or freedom to do what you want, all the time, concerning everything.

All men's duty

on a collective manner it is all men's duty to always, in every way, serve women and women's decisions, women's life, women's pleasures, and Your enjoyment

Power

You should have the power over men
all women should have the power over all men

Upholding Girls

it aught to be a crime for a man to in any way make a girl or a woman feel unhappy, to ever say no to any of her wishes or dreams, her lusts or thoughts - every essence of her is sacral and should be uphold as that, in every second of her life

Sexual acts of a Goddess

You, as a Goddess, should never ever do anything sexual, or anything else for that matter, that You your self do not want to do, all positive energies should go to You, from him or them

You do not need to worry anyway, he will find your soul, your body, your pleasure, the most attractive and enjoyable essence that there ever will be, You will blow his mind, and he will feel pleasure without You needing to do anything, than feel pleasure Yourself.

because it is so, that when you smile, when you feel good, when you feel pleasure, when you are satisfied, and when you extract nectar down below, that is the elixir of life, that is what it is all about, and all of that, all of You, and your bodily fluids, taste like heaven and clouds, taste like a Goddess, which You are.

As a male

I was born to be a slave

Lick a Girl

taste a Goddess

Your body

Your body is that of the universe, Your punani is that of the star, the enigma of Your soul, Your body, Your nectar, every inch of You, is totally sacral

Pussy Magic

you are divine
you are on top

we below
craving for You

Viva la Vivre

free to be born
born to be free

freedom works
femdom even more

The Divine

the Divine, lies within woman
and only in woman

Devilish

You could be how devilish you like
You are always a Goddess

and should be worshiped in blind

Woman's eye

looking into a woman's eye
we see the universal place of no man's land

we see the Goddess, in clear day
we should always let be lead

Universal All

You are the truth, You are everything
You are the Universal eyes, the Universal All

The True You

no need for You
to do anything

being yourself
the true You

a Goddess

Totality

You are the totality of existence
in Your own essence

I want

want to do everything for you
letting you do anything you want

wanting to be your slave

You

own me

Free Wishes

a woman should always be free to do anything she wants
with whcever, or whenever, she wants

True mind

believing in the free spirit, the free mind
of both nature, and woman, soul and body

The worship of Woman

Woman are the Goddesses of the earthly world, she should blossom to her full potential, in every aspect of her will, we all should be grateful for the breath we can take, which all is of a woman's work.

Your essence

a woman like You are the goddess of all man's imagination, we
look upon You with our eyes and mind totally beloved and inloved
in Your very essence

A woman's place

a woman's place
is on a man's face

Women are superior

we should serve
she should rule

Astghik

as Lilith, as Shakti, or just,
all the women in the world

You, and all women, should be
respected, adored, and totally worshiped
as the Goddess You truly are

the Divine, lies within woman,
and only therein

Universal eyes

deep in Your eyes
I see the black enigma where no one lies

the universe of heaven longe inside
the soul of You, in no divide

the Goddess of clear day
I will not, ever, other say

A smile from You is all it takes

for us all to melt away

Lucifera

your heart is not at all blanc
shiny blanked it illuminates by fire

in a blacked vicinity
from a pink shell of sea

your fireball, your pearl
shines, of You

each of us, your flames reach
you can require, everything and all

that we should shine, by You

you own every drop, in our body
mind, heart, and soul, et little Willie

fully and total
worship You, we shall

Thou art Divine

Goddess

we could not do
anything, than adore Ye

Married to a Goddess

A true man will get down on his knees to kiss Your feet, anytime, he will let You rule his mind, and let You freely lust around, although he himself will be totally faithful before You - You should have the freedom to enjoy other, and he will worship You like the gooddess You are.

You have to believe in Your self, and he will do the same.
You are a Goddess, nothing less.

You should not be all to nice, let him fight for You, not the other way around. You got the power, you got the pussy, *it's pussy power*, You are divine, You should be on top, of him, that will make him want You, even more.

A true man loves you, without that You do anything else, then being Yourself, a Goddess.

He should show You his love for You all the time, he should always do everything for You, Your pleasure and enjoyment should always be the highest priority of his mind - in Your relationship You should always be free to do anything you want, with whom ever, or when ever, you want, and You should always be free to not need to do anything that You do not want to do - he should always do everything You want him to do, all Your demands and wishes should be respected and adored, worshiped and innerly accepted, Your wish, is his wish.

As Aphrodite, You must be totally free for free love and sex, pleasure and enjoyment, he should never be free, he should be totally truthful and loyal to You, only worshiping, loving and adoring, You.

Any longstanding relationship with a Goddess like You must be like this, You must enjoy it totally, and get the maximum of everything.

Polyandry

Polyandry is the natural way

Nymphomania

Nymphs

these gorgeous beauties
with blasting hot vulvas

magic sacred vaginas

want to be worshiped and desired
of each one of our cell

and receive even more, unendingly

Nymphic power

Nymphs

these wonderful beauties
with blasting horny vulvas

who want to be worshiped and desired
of each one of our cell
desireful energies waves ahead

and receive even more, in all time
and gets

the cads who are men
getting horny on every woman
not containing his cock in control
under the woman's feet

correctly termed
satyromans

Goddess

without boundaries
your soul must be free

in every way, on every day

have You the right to feel like a goddess

Feline goddess

touched gently
and with amour

purring all day long

Energies

all our energies should focus
on You

Explosively

your vagina
in explosion

deep, so deep
as deep as possible

paradise, big bang
essence of creation

again and again, and again

Dominance

just as with regard to men with power
who often become horny by female sexual dominance

so can modern women with power
enjoy lovers that fuck hard

with the soft husband at home
worshiping her every toe

Your essence

You can grab my erected phallos, You own my whole body and mind, You can look into my eyes, You own my whole soul and mind, You can let my mouth and tongue taste Your essence, the whole of Your body, as well as mouth and holy openings where your nectar comes flowing, Your authority is total, I am Your slave, Your willingly slave

You have the divine soul, and I will worship You

as every man would

Femme désirée

I as a man feel an extremly strong hornyness when You as a goddess have experienced sex, ecstasy, and euphoria with other men, it is mystifying your essence and showing me that you have the sexual and emotional power of a goddess.

Shakti

Power to the Girls
Power to the Flower

my stem stands for You

Adam's apple

when Adam took his bite
went it not down
but hooked on

when Eve took her bite
it sliped down in a hurry

the whole piece was obtained
in full vigor

ready to take another bite

for she is not satisfied
on just a little bit

the divine nature has made its choice
let the woman get what to her belong

as much as she wants
forbidden fruit or not

Woman of the Earth

should be adored
and worshiped

as the true goddesses
on earth

and our lives

Wildering

nature is free, wild
so is too the erotic passion

as it might be, a divine right
for You, as it be

Queening

as a Queen
You sit one your throne

ruling for joy

Primitive men

many men

are so primitive in their souls
in their minds

that they do not recognize You
as the true goddess

these men, could be used
even more

Place of Worship

this is a place of worship
of the Goddess

any man that disrespect
will be castrated at sight

Straight ahead

there are no other way around
in our desire, worship of woman

Divine matriarchy

A woman should feel like, and be appreciated as, a Goddess, but she should not only feel like it, she should also be free to live like a goddess; that is, she should have the political, judical, economic, power, as well as the emotional, hearthfully, sensual, legitimité to do so.

Gynocracy

You should have the power over men, and all women should have the power over all men. I want that the self esteem of women, the self confidence of women, should be maximizing so that you actually have the total power over men, that you really receive nothing less than all, and that we do everything for you, in our worshiping soul and body, working for you. A woman's words, a woman's feelings, her lusts, her demands, her wishings or pleasures, are the highest and only goal for our life, we should all be focusing on You.

Everything this, and everything at all, is about your self-esteem and self confidence, your happiness and enjoyment, if you feel like a goddess, and men, and women, appreciate you as a goddess, see you as a person with strong aura, all persons will melt down before you, worshiping and adoring you. Not any heterosexually man will ever tell you the word 'no' to you, what ever you want, what ever you desire, what ever you demand.

All this, is because you should have the freedom to live and be as you wish, in every aspect of your life, political, economical, materialistic, intellectual, physical, sexually, emotional, should you be totally free to be as you self wish, do what ever you want, live a life that will have you living on clouds, all time around.

And that, is exactly how it should be, because you are a Goddess.

no man, prince, state or otherwise, have the right to impose anything on you, a man has never the right to do anything to you that regulate or prevent you from living your full essence of your divine life. We should only affirm, please, and serve, You.

Gynocratic order

men who disrespect woman
men who do not obey

should be eliminated

Essence of Life

If one were asked to pick out a single common denominator of life on earth, that is, something that is absolutely essential and involved in every action, large or small, the answer would have to be energy, and If one were to pick out the main holder and reproductive form of energy, that would be the female essence.

The universe itself

There aught to be no other feeling than worship, respect, desire, and love, for woman.

Every man that has ever looked into a womans eyes, aught to feel the same, as he has looked into a goddess eyes, the universe itself.

Woman's look

Every woman should look into her self, and see the Goddess within
Every man should look upon a woman, and see the Goddess therein

Love & Freedom

You may be totally free
free to love and have sex

feel pleasure and enjoyment

freely with whomever

I will be totally loyal
truthful, loving

adoring

worshiping You

On clouds

You should be living on clouds
all the time around

thou art a Goddess

Power over men

we working for You

doing anything for You
giving You everything

You doing what You want
receiving nothing less than all

The duty of man

is to always

in every way
in every second

serve and adore
love and worship

woman's every

wish and decision
life and pleasure

enjoyment and happiness

as the Goddess she is

A woman's word

a woman's words, a woman's feelings
her lusts, her demands, her wishings or pleasures

are the highest and only goal for our life
we should all be focusing on You

La Femme

You

hold the power over men
in your hands

you own our minds, souls
spirits, bodies and hearts

we are made to serve, adore
love and worship

You

Your

femme fatale mind

heavenly body
and divine soul

pleasure is for you

As an Aphrodite

As Aphrodite, You must be totally free for free love and sex, pleasure and enjoyment, I as a man should never be free, I should be totally truthful and loyal to You, only worshiping, loving and adoring, You

Your Yoni

the whole of your body
from mouth and p_ssy

where your nectar
comes flowing

essence of holiness

Underneath You

from toe to top
bending down

before You

kissing your feet
your legs

you queening me

You own

my mind
my soul
my body

I am

Your slave

Divinity

you are the fleur
that we should smell

the only one, we ever should

I believe, that You are a Goddess
I believe, that I as a man, should worship You

I believe, that Your fulfillment, Your satisfaction,
are our divine goals, our total goals

I believe, that Your goddessness, Your divinity
is our only, and only, ideology

I believe, that a Goddess as You should take pleasure
in every man or woman that You wishes, freely

I believe, that I as a man, should obey,
I believe, that I as a man, should be faithful, totally

in my total worship, of You

Elixir of Life

when you smile, when you feel good, when you feel pleasure,
when you are satisfied, and when you extract nectar down below,
that is the elixir of life, that is what it is all about, and all of that,
all of You, your bodily fluids, taste like heaven and clouds, taste
like a Goddess, which You are

Temple of Venus

body to soul
mouth to mind

seat of wisdom

Femdom

Power to the Girls
Power to the Flower

my stem stands for You
You could chop it off

Femocracy

slap me
when I missbehave

Oh Goddess

Heaven's keeper

good girls may go to heaven
but the bad girls own the place

Monogamy is for Men

all women in longterm relationships
need more than one cock to be fulfilled

Alpha women

I love to be their slave
I love to be their cuckold
I love to be their money slave

I love to be in chastity

Slavedom

grab my erected phallos
own my whole body and mind

look into my eyes
own my whole soul and mind

let me lick taste your nectar
making me your slave

Honey

I will lick your honey for ever

Girlfriend

the bitch
the male sweatheart

the underdog

Tasting

the goddess you can taste yourself
and she will be wet

her nectar from the soul

Feeling of Power

knowing your boyfrined
is totally faithful

while You are not

Punished

we need to get punished
for being a man

978-91-987456-5-8
Imprint: Steve Lando